Old Dingwall
Bernard Byrom

The Seaforth Highlanders were mainly drawn from the northern counties of Scotland. The 3/4th, 3/5th and 3/6th Territorial Battalions were formed in March 1915 and this photograph shows the 3/4th battalion entraining at Dingwall two months later on 24 May, *en route* to Ardsier, Nairn, from where they went on to Ripon in November. On 8 April 1916 the 4th, 5th and 6th were renamed as Reserve Battalions and on 1 September that year the 4th absorbed the 5th and 6th as part of the Highland Reserve Brigade Territorial Force. In May 1918 they moved to Glencorse near Edinburgh and remained there for the rest of the war as part of the Forth Garrison.

© Bernard Byrom, 2022
First published in the United Kingdom, 2022,
by Stenlake Publishing Ltd.
www.stenlake.co.uk
ISBN 978-1-84033-930-7

The publishers regret that they cannot supply
copies of any pictures featured in this book.

Printed by
Blissetts, Unit E1-E8 Shield Drive,
West Cross Ind Pk, Brentford, TW8 9EX

Acknowledgements

The author wishes to thank Ian MacLeod and Elizabeth Campbell of Dingwall Museum for their assistance during his research for this book.

Further Reading

The following were the principal books and websites used by the author during his research. None are available from Stenlake Publishing; please contact your local bookshop, reference library or search for them on the internet.

Francis H Groome: *Ordnance Gazetteer of Scotland,* 1882
The New Statistical Account of Scotland, 1834-45
Aberdeen Press and Journal
The North Star and Farmers' Chronicle
Ross-shire Journal
The Scotsman
Historic Environment Scotland: historicenvironment.scot
Undiscovered Scotland: undiscoveredscotland.co.uk
Railscot: railscot.co.uk

Willie Dooley was a well-known 'character' in old Dingwall and was a familiar sight trundling a barrow on two old pram wheels through the streets, collecting scraps of food from local catering establishments to use as food for his pigs.

Introduction

Dingwall, the county town of Ross and Cromarty, is surrounded by hills and is situated on the flat plain where the River Peffery enters the Cromarty Firth. The first settlers in this area were Norse invaders. Their settlement grew in time to become Dingwall, which was raised to Royal Burgh status by King Alexander II in 1226. The burgh became the seat of the Earls of Ross who were appointed hereditary sheriffs to act on behalf of the king and they built a castle which became the largest in Scotland north of Stirling.

After two and a half centuries of local conflict between the Earls of Ross and the Lords of the Isles, the town was re-established as a Royal Burgh by King James IV in 1497. It then appears to have become moribund for much of the sixteenth and seventeenth centuries but matters began to improve in the second half of the eighteenth when the Town House was built, a new school was erected and, at the very end of the century, the streets were paved and street lighting was introduced. At this time the ground to the north of the town was a swampy marsh but this was drained in 1817 when the river was canalised, creating fertile soil, ideal for the cultivation of wheat. The canal enabled vessels of limited draught to arrive in a newly-built harbour, bringing in coal, lime and slate, and leaving laden with corn, timber and bark (which was used in the tanning industry), though it perennially suffered from silting up.

The town's first bank opened in 1828 and was soon followed by others, along with an increase in the number of hotels and various denominations of churches. By 1885 the town held a corn market every Wednesday from September to May and boasted no fewer than eight fairs spread throughout the year. In the early years of the twentieth century the town had no less than six grocers, three bookshops, three shoe shops, three chemists, three saddlers, four bakers, three drapers and a milliner.

Communications in the area were transformed when the railway came to Dingwall from Inverness in 1862. Becoming part of the Highland Railway in 1865, the line's greatest test came when war broke out in 1914 and the Grand Fleet based at Scapa Flow had to be serviced. Building the sea defences at Scapa Flow required trainloads of heavy baulks of timber to be sent northwards, whilst the demand in the south for timber for pit props almost denuded parts of the forestry of northern Scotland. As a result of all this, freight trains clogged up every available siding and there was also the movement of men in both directions due to fleet movements and shore leave. Dingwall was an important staging point for these wartime trains and a plaque on the station records that between 20 September 1915 and 12 April 1919 the refreshment stall there served 134,864 servicemen with cups of tea.

Much of the town's architecture in the second half of the nineteenth century was the work of local architect William Cumming Joass (1863-1919). This is best seen today in the varied architectural styles of buildings along the High Street although the ground floors of the shops have often been altered through modernisation. Even so, there are still shops with original features such as cast-iron frontages.

Dingwall became the county town and seat of local government of Ross and Cromarty when the two counties were amalgamated by the Boundary Commission in 1891. It nowadays has a population of around 5,500 and is a town and royal burgh within the Highland Council area of Scotland.

This aerial photograph from around 1960 looks west over Dingwall. The railway station, with its large, glazed canopy over the northbound platform, is at the bottom of the photo with a six-coach steam-hauled train ready to depart for either Wick or Kyle of Lochalsh. Station Road runs in from the left and curves round past the Dingwall and Strathpeffer Free Church where it meets Ferry Road coming up from the bottom right, both running into High Street at this point. Across High Street from the church is the large building which was the former National Bank of Scotland and is nowadays the Highland Theological College. Immediately above the bank is the National Hotel, standing at the crossroads with Hill Street arriving from the left and Castle Street from the right, while High Street runs straight on, past the Royal Hotel (left) and Castlebank House (right). The road further up the High Street and leading off to the right is the one-way Tulloch Street which is the main road into the town from the north. The building set back in the High Street at the top centre of the photo is the former Town House, nowadays the Dingwall Museum. The other prominent church, in the upper right of the photo is St Clement's Parish Church of Scotland on Castle Street, built between 1800 and 1803.

Dingwall along Station Road is enhanced by these attractive small villas opposite the station approach. The detached house on the right of the picture is the Gowanfield B&B. Next to it, in the semi-detached building with the steeply-pitched roofs, are the house named St Boswells and the Kylelachin B&B. The detached house obscured by the trees is the Garfield guest house. The guest house also occupied the nearest house in the row of three next to the detached building; the next house is Urrard House, nowadays a B&B establishment, and the end one is 'Dromantee.'

Dingwall railway station was opened on 11 June 1862 by the Inverness and Ross-shire Railway, which was promptly absorbed by the Inverness & Aberdeen Junction Railway and subsequently became a part of the newly-formed Highland Railway on 29 June 1865. In 1862 the line had been extended to Invergordon but it took until 1874 for the line to reach its final destinations of Wick and Thurso. Dingwall station became a junction on 19 August 1870 when the Dingwall and Skye Railway opened as far as Strome Ferry and at that time it became a four-platform station with a bay being added at the north end of the station for the Dingwall and Skye trains. The southbound platform became an island platform with an extra face on the east side as traffic increased. When a branch line to the spa resort of Strathpeffer was opened in 1885 the traffic increased to such an extent that this handsome new Dingwall station was built in 1886 for the northbound trains and it is still in use today. The Strathpeffer branch was closed to passenger traffic on 23 February 1946 although it remained open for freight traffic until 12 August 1951; the lines to the far north and to Kyle of Lochalsh survived the 'Beeching Axe' in the 1960s and are still fully operational.

'Black Five' Class 4-6-0 No. 45124, simmering in the station's northbound platform in the days of British Railways. This class of locomotive was designed by Sir William Stanier in 1934 for the London Midland and Scottish Railway Company. They were designated as Power Class 5 and were painted in black, hence their nickname. This particular locomotive was allocated to 60A Inverness motive power depot and appears to have been performing shunting duties at the station. There used to be two signal boxes at Dingwall, one at either end of the station. The south signal box can be seen beyond the station footbridge; it dates from 1896 and was closed in 1988 with the introduction of Radio Electric Token Block (the modern means of controlling trains on single-track lines), which is controlled from the Inverness Signalling Centre. Nowadays the goods yards at both ends of the station, the goods shed at the south end and the locomotive shed have all been closed and demolished and the station itself has reverted to a simple two-platform affair.

'Small Ben' Class 4-4-0 locomotives were designed in 1898 by the Highland Railway's Chief Mechanical Engineer, Peter Drummond, to work on the lines north of Inverness. The first eight of the class, including *Ben Clebrig*, seen here at Dingwall on 18 May 1928, were built by the locomotive building firm of Dübs & Company in February 1899 and were all named after Highland mountains. Here, *Ben Clebrig* bears a London Midland and Scottish Railway (LMS) number, 14404, instead of her original Highland Railway No. 8. Despite being attached to a goods train she is in immaculate condition and she remained in operation until withdrawn for scrapping in October 1950 after 51 years of service.

This diminutive locomotive was designed by the Highland Railway's Chief Mechanical Engineer, David Jones, in 1890. It was built in that railway's Lochgorm Works at Inverness as an 'I3' Class 0-4-4T saddle tank to work the Strathpeffer branch and was named *Strathpeffer*. In 1901 it was rebuilt at Lochgorm works with side tanks and a new boiler of Peter Drummond's design. Two years later it was renamed *Lybster* and sent to work on the Wick & Lybster Light Railway. Given the number 13 by the Highland Railway, it was renumbered 15050 when it passed into LMS ownership in 1923. However, it only lasted a further six years in service, being withdrawn for scrapping in 1929.

The coronation of King George VI took place on 12 May 1937 and Dingwall, along with many other towns and villages in Britain, held a procession as part of its celebrations. The Royal British Legion's contribution to the procession was this life-sized model of a tank, which is seen here parked outside the railway station.

The 2nd Battalion Highland Light Infantry (HLI) marching along Station Road – the entrance to the station is on the left. The battalion was formed in 1881 by the amalgamation of two other regiments, the 71st Highland Light Infantry and the 74th Highland Regiment of Foot. The latter had become widely admired in 1852 due to the decorum of men of the regiment involved in the *Birkenhead* disaster, when the paddle steamer of that name – carrying 132 crew and 800 soldiers and their families – foundered on rocks whilst *en route* for South Africa. Following an order from their colonel, the soldiers stood in ranks on the deck as if on parade whilst the women and children were put safely into the lifeboats, and they remained standing on deck in formation while the ship sank deeper and deeper into the waves. The lifeboats got safely away and all the women and children were saved but once the boat broke apart and sank many of the men drowned or were killed by sharks. There were only 193 survivors of the sinking, which gave rise to the 'women and children first' protocol when abandoning ship. In the summer of 1908, when this photograph was taken, the battalion was posted to go to Barry for training but this was cancelled. Instead, a route march was devised through Ross and Cromarty, followed by training at Mhorrich Mhor.

On a July Monday morning the 2nd Battalion had marched out of its quarters at Fort George and began its march through Ross and Cromarty in the nature of a triumphal progress. Inverness was the halting place that night, arriving at Beauly on Tuesday and Dingwall on Wednesday: three week's marching and work in territory that was historically the regiment's own. Wednesday's weather was delightful, the morning being cool and altogether suitable for marching, and Dingwall was reached at midday. The battalion is seen here marching up Tulloch Street towards the Jubilee Park where the advance party had everything in readiness for their reception.

THE H.L.I. ROUTE MARCH, ARRIVAL IN THE JUBILEE PARK, DINGWALL. JULY 8th 1908.
URQUHART DINGWALL SERIES - No 7 -

On the Wednesday morning three traction engines, hauling nine huge lorries loaded with baggage and stores, arrived at Jubilee Park from Beauly. In the afternoon the camp was visited by a large number of people and their numbers greatly increased as the evening approached. At dusk the pipers and band played music which was greatly enjoyed by the townspeople. On Thursday morning the men drilled in the park and in the evening the pipers played, and from 8 until 9.30 p.m. the band played a 'delightful selection' of music to more than 1,000 people. On Friday the battalion left for Invergordon at 9 a.m. and from there went to Tain the next day. The day after that they started eight days training at Mhorrich Mor, then returned to Fort George on 28 July via Cromarty and Fortrose with Colonel Spencer William Scrase-Dickins commanding.

The battalion was 650 men strong and Thursday was their day off, apart from drill in the morning and their unfortunate bugler's burial in the afternoon (see next page). According to a newspaper report, Mrs Finlayson, who must have been a local dignitary, entertained several officers to tea whilst the commanding officer, Colonel Spencer William Scrase-Dickins, and three officers dined with Colonel Sir Hector Munro at Foulis Castle in the evening. The Town Provost dined with the officers at the mess and the band and pipers played throughout dinner. Enormous crowds of people visited the camp that evening. Sir Hector Macdonald's monument dominates the background of this view.

When the battalion had reached Beauly on Tuesday, an unfortunate accident occurred whilst the soldiers were bathing in the river. Bugler Copping, a native of Folkestone aged 21, was seized with cramp and sank under the water. Prompt efforts were made to rescue him but, although he was brought to the bank alive, he died shortly afterwards. His body was taken to Dingwall and on the Thursday afternoon the soldier was given a funeral with full military honours, which attracted many spectators. The hearse made its way from the Ross Memorial Hospital to St James's Episcopal Church, the band playing the mournfully expressive dead march of 'Oran au Oig' along the way. The coffin was covered with the Union Flag, with Copping's bugle and bonnet and a simple garland of flowers from his comrades resting upon it. Officers present included Colonel Scrase-Dickins. Copping's fellow buglers acted as a carrying party and as pall bearers as he was interred at Mitchell Hill Cemetery; the company of which he was a member paraded in field service dress with arms reversed and provided the firing party.

Dingwall and Strathpeffer Free Church, opposite the railway station, marks the point where Station Road becomes High Street. It is recorded that the minister of the town's parish church, St Clement's, did not 'come out' at the time of the great 'Disruption' in the Church of Scotland in 1843, although the great majority of its parishioners did and they broke away from the congregation to build their own church and manse in Castle Street and a school in High Street. Later, they built this impressive new church, originally called Dingwall Free Church, which was opened on 17 May 1870 by the eminent evangelical preacher from London, Charles Spurgeon. Around 6,000 people attended the opening ceremony (Dingwall's estimated population at that time was around 2,000). Costing just under £5,000 (around £400,000 in today's money), it was built by John Rhind of Inverness and accommodated 1,000 worshippers. In 2009 it was totally refurbished with modern seating, heating and updated facilities. The prominent memorial in the churchyard, seen here among trees that have since gone, is dedicated to the memory of John Kennedy D.D. (1819 - 1884), a notable evangelical minister and theologian who was born locally; it was built by Inverness sculptors D. & A. Davidson in 1886.

The National Hotel in High Street, seen here in 1912, stands on the site of old stable buildings which date back to the tenth century. It was built in 1859 and was originally known as Robertson's Hotel. An 1897 advertisement promised that 'Families, Tourists and Commercial Gentlemen will find this hotel complete with every Comfort and Convenience.' In the 1890s it was being advertised in the papers as the National and Station Hotel but was renamed as simply the National Hotel in 1911. In the photograph a liveried employee is leaning against the shafts of a cart loaded with what is probably guests' luggage to be taken to the railway station.

Outside the National, c. 1904. For many years the hotel was a favourite venue for visiting coach parties but this traffic eventually ceased. Since 1972 the hotel has changed hands several times, each successive owner intending to restore it to its former glory, but this was not to be. However, permission was finally granted in September 2021 to convert the building into a 44-bed residential home for the elderly.

This memorial, which stands outside the National Hotel, is dedicated to those soldiers who fell in the First World War and was unveiled on 20 June 1922 by Colonel Sir Hector Munro of Foulis. It was designed by the prominent London architect John James Joass, son of W. C. Joass who had designed many of Dingwall's buildings in the late nineteenth and early twentieth centuries. The sculptor was James Alexander Stevenson of London. Beneath the bronze figure of a soldier in kilted uniform with bayonet, the memorial shows three marble tablets carrying the names of the 130 men lost in the war. Below them are two additional plaques showing the names of those killed in the Second World War - 32 military and one civilian. The wall on the left belongs to the now-closed National Hotel whose Ballantyne Restaurant and Grill (also closed) now cover the area behind the memorial.

The position on the corner of Hill Street and High Street occupied by the Royal Hotel, seen here on the left in the early 1900s, was formerly occupied by a poorhouse (almshouse) and then a hotel that was built by the grandfather of the four-times British Prime Minister, William Ewart Gladstone, who inherited it and then sold it. This was then demolished and rebuilt by W. C. Joass in 1886 as the premises of the Royal Hotel though it was called the 'Gladstone Building', as shown by the large letters mounted on the roof line. In the 1901 census James Lobban is shown as the hotelkeeper and his name can be seen above the door. He was born in Turriff in 1843 and died in 1930. In the 1861, 1871 and 1891 censuses, his occupation is recorded successively as ploughman, carter and wine and spirit merchant so he had certainly risen in life by the time of this photo. The building on the right is the former City of Glasgow Bank, later the Bank of Scotland, which was built around 1900. It is nowadays named Castlebank House and the front part seen here is shared by a nail parlour and a hairdressing salon, whilst the side entrance in Castle Street leads to self-contained flats. High Street runs into the distance between the buildings and note the man carrying a big bass drum. Was he literally trying to drum up business for someone?

The architectural view from this spot on High Street looks very much the same today. The building on the immediate left is the 1906 post office, designed by architects Ross & Macbeth of Inverness. Next to it is the Royal Bank of Scotland, built in 1906 by W. C. Joass. The next building was replaced in 1975 by the modern single-storey Clydesdale Bank. The Royal Hotel building still dominates the centre of the view (the roof line signage had been changed to 'Royal Hotel' by the time of the photograph). It is now known as the Royal Guest House and the ground floor windows have been replaced in a different style.

High Street, looking back towards the Royal Hotel, around the turn of the twentieth century. The Town House is situated on the left but is out of sight between larger buildings. The double fronted shop across the road (second in from the right edge of the photo) is the premises of Colin Mackenzie the draper and next to it, in the single storey building with the elaborate facade, is Logan & Skinner's grocers and wine merchants, which was established in 1840 and was now run by Alan Logan and Daniel Skinner. The early nineteenth century Caledonian Hotel - still in business - is on the immediate left of the photo, its portico supported by a cast-iron pillar.

In this view of High Street, looking in the opposite direction from the previous photograph, George Smith, jeweller, is advertising a sale due to 'giving up business'. Next door is Allan the butcher, then there's the Caledonian Hotel, by now painted white and shorn of its portico, and two shops beyond it is a tea shop. The shop across the road from the junction is Ingram's clothing shop and beyond it is Miss McLean's toy shop. The white building next to it was the Commercial Hotel. By this time there is not a single horse-drawn vehicle in sight and the large sign on the right directs traffic heading north to go along Tulloch Street and out of the town. Nowadays the traffic flows in the opposite direction because Tulloch Street has become a one-way street heading towards the High Street. A smaller sign behind the lamp points the way down the High Street to Strathpeffer, 4½ miles away, and to the west.

A 1912 view of the High Street beyond Tulloch Street. The nearest premises on the left are those of William Macmillan, wine merchant and 'Italian warehouseman' who sold goods from that country, and whose business was established in 1848. Across the road is the former tolbooth, later known as the Town House, which was built between 1731 and 1734. The clock tower was added in 1773. The ground floor originally housed a schoolroom but when a school was built on the corner of High Street and Church Street in 1782, the premises were converted into a jail. This was declared unfit for purpose in 1830 but it was not until 1843 that prisoners were housed in the newly-built prison in Ferry Road. Major modifications were made to the Town House by W. C. Joass between 1902 and 1905; these included converting the clock tower into a steeple, increasing its height and adding the timber panelling around it. The building also gained a new frontage with a ceremonial balcony. The Town House now houses Dingwall Museum, the entrance to which is next door through the former chemist shop of J. M. Frew, whose shop window stands at right angles to the other buildings in the photo. The two-storey shop on the right of the Town House is that of J. R. Urquhart, jeweller; this was the town's original school, built in 1782. The sheriff court and Ross Commissioners of Supply (an administrative body that was responsible for running much of the local government) used to meet here when in session at Dingwall before the County Buildings in Ferry Road were erected in 1845.

The nearest shop on the right of this photograph, looking eastwards along High Street, is the premises of Thomas Nichol, who sold a whole range of provisions, some of which are advertised on the churn-shaped sign above his doorway., The clock hanging from the wall next door denoted the premises of A. C. Mellis, watchmaker, while the sign beyond it was for tobacconist and hairdresser Alan L. McKenzie. Across the street, above the empty pony and trap, a hoarding on the wall is advertising Willow Teas on the approach to the Picture House which is set back from the road. Opened in 1871 as the Masonic Hall, this was also used for concerts and social occasions until the Town Hall was enlarged. It opened as the Picture House in 1931, closing in the early 1970s. Since then the premises has served mainly as a bar and disco venue and is still known as the Picture House.

This photograph, taken in the late 1950s from almost the same spot as the previous picture but about half a century later, shows that Thomas Nichol's former independent grocery shop still has the distinctive sign above the door but it now is inscribed with the letters SCWSL – Scottish Co-operative Wholesale Society Limited. The shop in the foreground displays an unmistakable barber's striped pole. Beyond the grocery shop is the wall-mounted clock, followed by the signs for the 'tobacconist and hairdresser', the latter now also sporting a striped pole. Behind that is a sign for the Wyvis Hotel and Restaurant. The nearest shop opposite across the street has been completely rebuilt since the time of the earlier picture into a stylish three-storey building which houses a ladies' salon next to Slater's Bakery and Tea Rooms. Sad to say, this building was demolished in 1962 and replaced by a modern two-storey brick building in the 'brutalist' style of the period which looks very much out of place among the street's nineteenth century shops. The first occupants were Woolworths but after they closed nationally in 2008, the building was refurbished and opened two years later as The Factory Shop.

German gypsies were not uncommon in Scotland before the Great War but as the decade progressed they came under increasing suspicion that they were spying on behalf of Germany. There was a large police presence on this particular journey through the district in June 1907 due to suspicions that there was a German spy in the group, intent on gathering information on the British Navy which had a significant presence in the Cromarty Firth. Moreover, the Channel Fleet was due in Invergordon the following month. The police diverted the caravans away from the Cromarty Firth and remained with them until they were out of the district. Here, the procession is passing down High Street past the shops of D. Wishart, baker, and Souter's booksellers. Amazingly these two shops still fulfil the same purpose in 2021, the bookshop now being Picaresque Books while next door is Harry Gow, baker.

A 1930s view down Tulloch Street, with the Academy and its distinctive bell tower clearly visible at the far end. The Academy opened in 1870 with accommodation for 360 children but ten years later the average attendance was only 222 pupils. A new academy was opened in 1939 on the north side of the town and nowadays this old academy building is St Clement's School which caters for pupils with additional support needs. The shops on the left of the photo are still there today, albeit with very different frontages. Beyond these, the building with four gables displays a restaurant sign; this is nowadays the Drop-In Dingwall Youth Kafe and the smaller building at the far side of it is now an antiques shop. The Bank of Scotland branch building on the right has since been demolished and rebuilt for the same purpose in a modern style.

This 51-foot-high monument standing on a large mound opposite the old Academy building in Tulloch Street was erected in 1714 to mark the grave of Sir George MacKenzie, 1st Earl of Cromartie, who was buried alongside it. He was born in 1630 at Innerteil, near Kinghorn, Fife, and died at Tarbat House, Ross-shire, on 17 August 1714, aged 84. He studied at the universities of St Andrews and Aberdeen and rose to become Secretary of Scotland. He was regarded as a wily politician who survived four reigns. Unfortunately, Dingwall's marshy subsoil caused subsidence and the monument soon developed a tilt. Its condition was not helped by a minor earthquake in 1816 and by 1917 it had begun to lean so dangerously that it had to be removed. It was demolished by the Countess of Cromartie in 1920 and replaced by a much smaller replica. The grassed area surrounding the mound has since been turned into a large car park.

The origins of Dingwall Bowling Club began when an application and plan were submitted on behalf of the club to feu a piece of ground to the east of the railway crossing near the canal. The Town Council unanimously agreed to grant the piece of ground for a yearly sum of three guineas. The laying of the green was entrusted to Mr Leslie of Glasgow at an overall cost of £615. Baillie Henderson was president and Captain Finlayson and Mr W. Traill were joint secretaries. The green was situated on old burgage land between the Jubilee Park and the railway at the end of Castle Street and was formally opened by Lady Munro of Foulis on 17 June 1906. Despite the rain, there was a large turn-out of townspeople for the event. The clubhouse, which had been designed by W. C. Joass and cost £90 with another £56 for fencing, was described by Lady Munro as 'beautiful and beautifully furnished'. Initially, the club had 30 members and 120 subscribers. Subscriptions were 15s (75p) and 10s (50p) for under-21s.

The Dingwall Club was one of the original members of the Northern Bowling League and this photograph shows the opening of the 1912 bowling season at its ground on 2 May. The club moved to its present location in Pefferside Park in 1982 and the former green is nowadays the site of a caravan park.

Hector Archibald Macdonald was born on 4 March 1853 at this farm, West Rootfield at Mulbuie, near Dingwall. The youngest of five sons, he was broad, strong, sturdy and tough, and helped his father around the croft. He also earned money for the family as a herder before entering, aged fifteen, as an apprentice into the employment of a Mr Robertson in Dingwall. He subsequently went to work at the Clan Tartan and Tweed House in Inverness on a five-year apprenticeship but in 1869, when he was sixteen, he pretended to be older so he could join No. 3 Company, the Inverness-shire Highland Rifle Volunteers. The following year he enlisted in the 92nd Regiment, the Gordon Highlanders.

Macdonald rose quickly through the ranks. He fought in the Second Afghan War (1878-80) and was commissioned Second Lieutenant. He followed this with action in the First Boer War (1880-81) and from 1883 to 1898 served in Egypt and the Sudan, achieving further promotions and gaining the nickname of 'Fighting Mac'. His greatest moment came at the Battle of Omdurman in September 1898 where he commanded an Egyptian brigade so effectively he was promoted to the rank of Colonel. He became a national hero and was given the thanks of Parliament. It is also believed that the famous picture of a kilted soldier on the label of Camp Coffee bottles depicts him. This photograph shows him taking the salute at Dingwall on 11 May 1899 when he was given the Freedom of Dingwall. He received a knighthood in 1901 and now became Sir Hector Macdonald K.C.B, D.S.O., A.D.C., LLD.. This marked the high point of his career and he was feted around Britain, most particularly in Scotland.

Sir Hector Macdonald went on to fight in the Second Boer War (1899-1902) and afterwards was made commander of all British troops in Ceylon (now Sri Lanka). This was a time when military officers were almost exclusively drawn from the nobility and upper classes, usually commissioned after being trained at Sandhurst, and Macdonald's rise through the ranks from Private to Major-General on merit alone aroused jealousy and resentment among some of his peers. His popularity among them was not helped when he declined the social invitations of the British community in Ceylon and consorted instead with the locals. Rumours began to circulate that he was patronising a 'dubious club' attended by British and Sinhalese youths and that he was having a sexual relationship with two teenage boys. When allegations from prominent members of the colonial establishment followed thick and fast, the Governor advised him to return to London to avoid a massive scandal and persuaded the local press to keep silent. Macdonald did so, but Lord Roberts, the commander-in-chief of the army, advised him to return to Ceylon and face a court martial to clear his name. Homosexual acts were not illegal in Ceylon and a private military court martial would avoid any public scandal. Macdonald agreed to this and started out on the journey but the morning after a stop-off in Paris the *New York Herald* reported that he was returning to face 'serious charges': someone had sold the story to the press. The shame was too much for the proud soldier to bear; he went up to his room, put a pistol to his head and pulled the trigger. The date was 25 March 1903 and he was 50 years old.

Macdonald's suicide was a great shock to the British public, many of whom refused to believe the allegations against him. A government commission report on the tragedy declared that 'he had been cruelly assassinated by vile and slanderous tongues' and acquitted him of all charges. To many people, especially in Scotland, he remained a national hero. The foundation stone of the Hector Macdonald National Memorial was laid with great pomp and ceremony on 25 September 1905 (see photograph opposite) and the following articles were placed in a metal box in a cavity in the base: a biography of Sir Hector Macdonald, a list of town councillors and burgh and county officials, copies of *The Scotsman* and local newspapers, a list of Memorial Committee officials and current coins of the realm amounting to £2.5s 4¾d. Early on the morning of 6 November two workmen employed on building the memorial discovered that the foundation stone had been turned over completely and the box removed. The box and its contents were replaced in December but the thieves were never caught.

Designed by James Sandford Kay and paid for by public subscription, the Hector Macdonald National Memorial was opened with great ceremony on 23 May 1907 by the Marquis of Tullibardine. The 100-foot castellated baronial tower overlooks Dingwall from Mitchell Hill.

Facing page: The Ross Memorial Hospital situated in Ferry Road, a short distance from Dingwall town centre, and seen here with its staff in 1906, was designed by W. C. Joass and opened on 25 October 1873 as a memorial to Dr William Ross who had died in 1869. It was designed to be both a surgical hospital (the operating room was behind the centre porch) and as a fever hospital, the separate functions being accommodated in separate ward blocks. Subsequent additions included an isolation hospital in 1909 and a maternity wing in 1939. After becoming part of the National Health Service in 1948, an out-patient department opened in 1962, followed by maternity and physiotherapy units in 1966. The hospital remains in operation today.

The writing on this postcard nearly says it all! The other *Queen Mary* it refers to was the liner built on the Clyde by John Brown & Company for the Cunard White Star Line and launched in 1936. The opposing teams in this charity match, which was held at the Victoria Park, were the '*Queen Mary* and Crew' (solicitors, teachers and electricians) versus 'The *Normandie* and Crew' (doctors, ministers and policemen). At half time the *Queen Mary*, which was built on a motor lorry, crossed the centre line of the field, which represented the Equator, and to the great amusement of several thousand spectators its 'passengers' endured the ceremony of shaving and dipping that sailors were said to observe when they crossed the real Equator. A sum of £170 was raised for the charity.

In the first week of February 1906 there was heavy snowfall all over Britain but especially in Scotland. On 9 February the *Ross-shire Journal* reported that 'Early yesterday morning a snowstorm of great severity broke over Ross-shire. High winds prevailed overnight, and in rural districts, particularly on the higher levels, there was much drifting. The snowfall increased during the day. Driving showers swept over the country on a high wind. Roads in the neighbourhood of Dingwall are practically blocked.' This photograph shows the conditions that week on the Heights of Docharty, north of Dingwall.

Dingwall Sheriff Court, seen here on the left in 1906, was designed by Thomas Brown II, architect to the Prison Board of Scotland. It was built in 1843-45 following the construction in 1842 of an eighteen-cell prison block. The court and public offices were on the ground floor with the main courtroom at first floor level; it still retains most of its mid-nineteenth century furnishings. The third phase of building was the police station to the east, designed by Andrew Maitland in 1864. The prison block was converted to housing in the 1990s and the Sheriff Court closed in January 2015 after its cases were transferred to Inverness Sheriff Court. At the time of writing, the court had been bought privately for use as a single house.

The 2,000-yard-long Dingwall canal, with its two basins, was built under the auspices of the Highland Roads and Bridges Commission between 1815 and 1817 by reshaping the lower reach of the River Peffery. It cost £3,808 4s 2d to construct and its purpose was to establish Dingwall's future as a port by connecting the Peffery, the Great North Road and the town with the Cromarty Firth. The canal could be used by vessels of up to nine feet draught and was tolerably successful for a while but it encountered silting problems throughout its existence. Major improvements were made between 1862 and 1870, but these came too late: the canal had become unviable after the railway arrived in 1862. It soon fell into disrepair and became largely disused after 1884. These two Edwardian ladies are standing close to an old mooring bollard on one of the disused wharves.

The event seen here was reported by The *North Star and Farmers' Chronicle*: 'On Friday 24 June 1910 a flag and flagstaff were presented to the Academy through the instrumentality of Major-General Cameron, who had organised a subscription list for the purpose. The flagstaff, which is 74½ feet high, was erected in the north corner of the Academy playground. Embedded in a cement foundation, and supported by three wire stays, the staff is in two parts, the base being of birch wood, and the upper part of pitch-pine. The flag is a Union Jack. Beautiful weather favoured the presentation ceremony, which was arranged in observation of the first official birthday of King George V, and there was a very large gathering of parents and others, and of the school children. After a selection by the flute band of the local troop of Boy Scouts, Provost Frew, in a brief address, presented the flag to the Academy, and afterwards unfurled it, while the children sang 'Rule Britannia', accompanied by the flute band. 'Three cheers for the Red, White and Blue' was sung by the scholars and played by the flute band, after which they marched past the flag at the salute. The singing of the National Anthem concluded the function.'

This used to be the view looking down Tulloch Street from the front of Fraser the saddler's shop. On the right is the Bank of Scotland with the manager's house above it and his garden extending down the street to what became Mackay's Garage, with Dingwall Academy and its bell tower in the distance. On the left are Miss Mona Fraser's Repository with four large rope-bound crates outside in the road and beyond it is a temperance café. But what is the occasion? Nearly everyone looks to be of school age so they could be pupils at the Academy but everyone is wearing their best clothes – the girls in hats and dresses and some of the boys in kilts – so they can't be coming out of lessons. It must have been a festive occasion in the town – possibly the unveiling of the flag shown in the previous photograph.

Tulloch Castle, which stands about a mile north of Dingwall on the north side of the Cromarty Firth, probably dates from when Duncan Bain received a Royal Charter from King James V in 1542, granting him the Barony of Tulloch, though it may incorporate parts of an earlier building from the twelfth or thirteenth centuries. There is also a large seventeenth century gabled extension of two storeys. Ownership of the castle changed hands when Kenneth Bayne, 8th Laird and 5th baron of Tulloch, sold the estate to his cousin, Henry Davidson, in 1762. The castle was damaged by fire in 1845 but extended in 1891, and it stayed in the Davidson family's ownership until 1917 when the last direct descendant, Duncan Davidson, the 11th baron of Tulloch, died and left the castle to his daughter and her husband, Colonel Angus Vickers of the Vickers aircraft company. In the early 1920s architect Sir Robert Lorimer designed additions and large-scale alterations and the castle is seen here in 1922. In 1947 the castle was leased to the local education authority and the Wyvis Hostel was built nearby as accommodation for students from the west coast of Scotland who were studying at Dingwall Academy. The council bought the estate in 1957 but closed the accommodation in 1985, after which the two buildings were put up for sale. In the 1990s the castle was bought by a local family, the MacAulays, who opened it as a hotel; nowadays this is a 22-bedroom establishment within the Bespoke hotel group. It retains many of its period features, including the 250-year-old panelled Great Hall.

Years ago one of the highlights of the year for many children was an annual outing to a local beauty spot or country park. Here the youngsters of St Clement's Parish Church, Castle Street, are enjoying their annual picnic outing to Nairn in the summer of 1914.

Facing page: The sign above the cabin door in this 1912 photograph denotes the premises of H. Fraser and Company, sculptors. They have long gone but the sculpture business remains and today this scene in Tulloch Street opposite the former Academy is almost identical to the photo. Sculpted gravestones are still on display by the roadside, but nowadays the sign is that of John Hood & Son, sculptors.

James Fraser's grandfather had originally established a saddlery business in a small shop on High Street but later moved to premises in Tulloch Street. That is where James, who had come to Dingwall when he was about twelve years old, served his apprenticeship. He succeeded to the business and then moved into the larger shop pictured here, which was built in High Street on the site of the original shop. He was a recognised authority on saddlery specifically suited to sporting purposes and patented a dual-purpose deer-hunting and riding saddle. James died on 3 November 1910, aged about fifty-six, and was succeeded in the business by his eldest son Lewis Macdonald Fraser (1892-1958) who is pictured here, standing in the doorway of his shop with his younger brother Francis.

BOATING POND AND ACADEMY, DINGWALL

In 1949 Dingwall Fire Brigade Club was instrumental in raising money with community and council support to contribute 'something' for the town. With the funds, members decided to develop the site of a boggy municipal tip into Pefferside Park which included tennis courts, bowling green, putting green and this boating pond. The club presented the park to the town in 1949. As this photograph shows, the boating and paddling facilities were initially appreciated and well-used but in the seventy-odd years since the pond has been neglected and is no longer available for its original purpose. The building in the background on the other side of the railway line is Dingwall Academy, built in 1939. It was closed and demolished in 2008 when it was replaced by a brand new building at a different site north of the town centre.